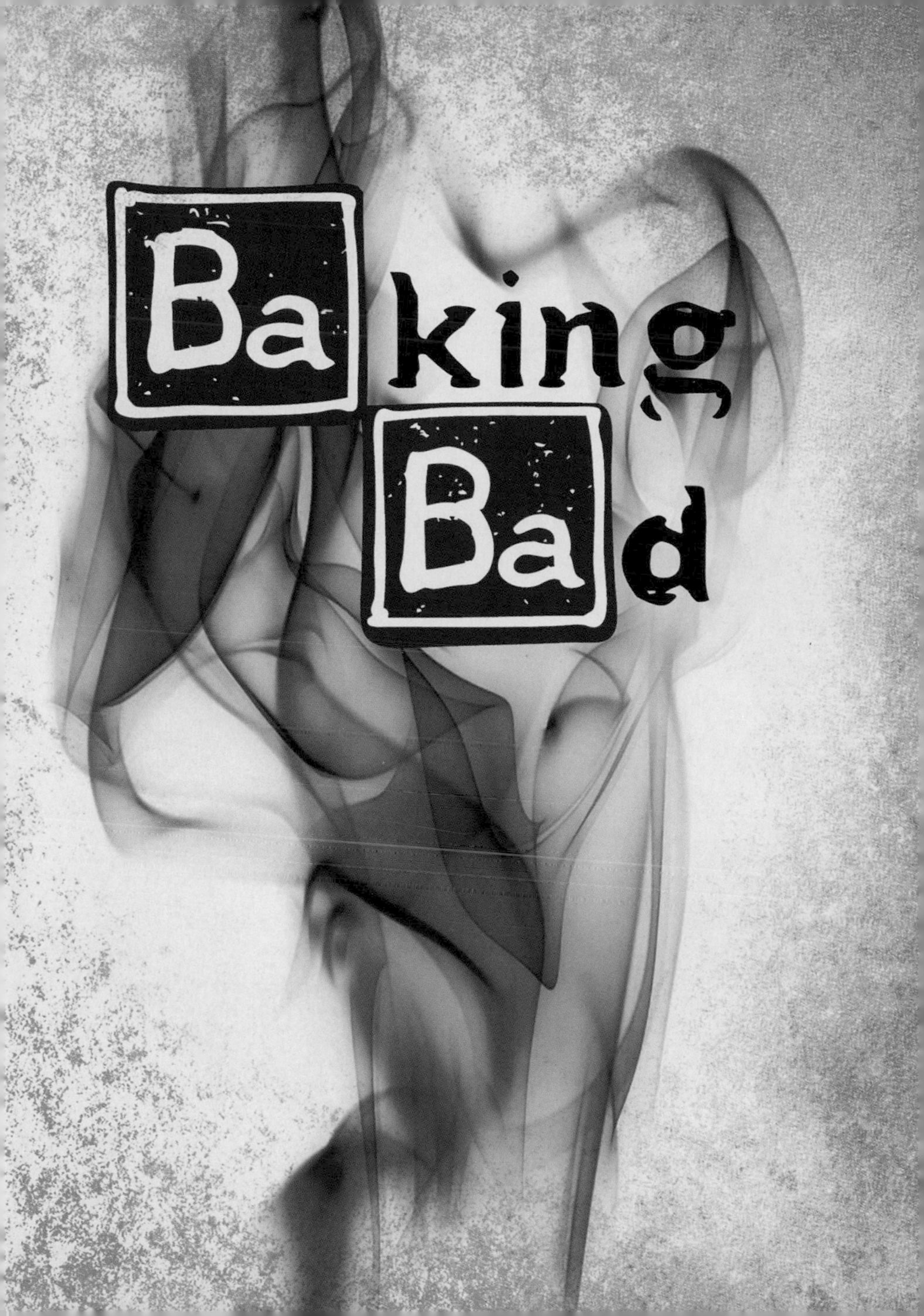
Baking
Bad

£1·50
23/4/18

14 bakeries between Nevada and Albuquerque

Hiding in plain sight
since 1989!

Baking Bad

Great Recipes.
No Meth-In Around.

Walter Wheat

This edition first published in Great Britain in 2014 by
Orion
an imprint of the Orion Publishing Group Ltd
Orion House, 5 Upper St Martin's Lane,
London WC2H 9EA
An Hachette UK Company

3 5 7 9 10 8 6 4 2

A CIP catalogue record for this book is available
from the British Library.

Hardback ISBN: 978 1 4091 5756 4

Printed in Italy

The Orion Publishing Group's policy is to use papers that are natural, renewable and recyclable and made from wood grown in sustainable forests. The logging and manufacturing processes are expected to conform to the environmental regulations of the country of origin.

Every effort has been made to fulfil requirements with regard to reproducing copyright material. The author and publisher will be glad to rectify any omissions at the earliest opportunity.

"Breaking Bad" is a registered trademark of Sony Pictures Television Inc. This book is not associated with or endorsed by Sony Pictures Television Inc. or any other third parties.

www.orionbooks.co.uk

Leaves of Grass.

TO J.S.

IT'S AN HONOUR
WORKING WITH YOU.
FONDLY

W.W.

CONTENTS

SEASON 3

SEASON 4

SEASON 5

INTRODUCTION

I AM THE ONE WHO BAKES.

Who are you talking to right now? Whose voice is
it you think you're reading? Do you know how many
cupcakes I make in a year? Each of them so
miraculously light and moreish it would blow
your mind! Even if I told you, you wouldn't believe
me. Do you know what would happen if I suddenly
decided to stop baking? A business the size of
Krispy Kreme goes belly up. Disappears! It ceases
to produce delicious doughy treats without me.
No, you clearly don't know who you're talking to.
So, let me enlighten you. A guy opens his door to
receive a batch of cookies still warm from the
oven, and you think that of me?
No. I am the one who bakes.

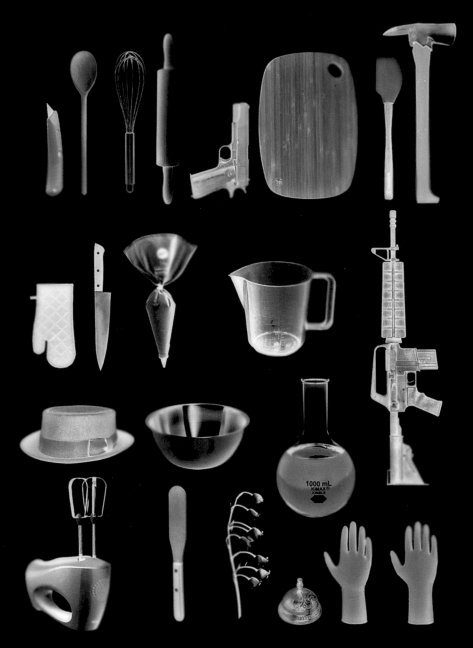

NO HALF MEASURES

If you're serious about getting into the empire business,
you're going to need these...

HOW PURE IS YOUR BAKE?

There's a lot of product out there, and only the purest, bluest shit will earn the money you need to provide for your family.

Not everyone can be a Heisenberg from the get-go, though. Use this key to work out your baking level. The lower the percentage, the easier the bake.

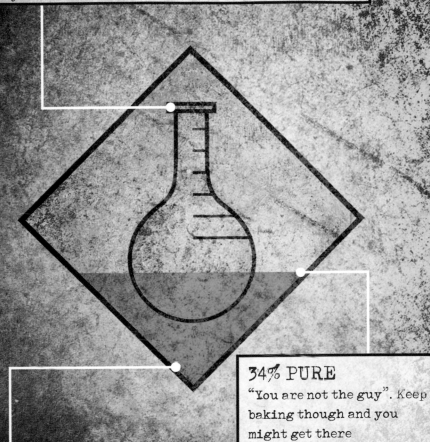

98% PURE

"Say my name". You are a legendary baker. Your product so blue the market will pay whatever you ask

34% PURE

"You are not the guy". Keep baking though and you might get there

7% PURE

"You are an insane, degenerate piece of filth and you deserve to die"

SEASON 1

MR WHITE'S TIGHTY WHITEY BITES

44% PURE

Who would have thought tighty whities and a green shirt could ever be a good look? It's early days (maybe it's even your pilot bake) so these delicious cookies are sweet and warm, but give them time and they'll mature into something much darker and more complex

INGREDIENTS

FOR THE GINGERBREAD:

12oz/350g all-purpose flour
2 tsp (10ml) baking powder
2 tsp (10ml) ground ginger (or more to taste)
4oz/100g cold butter
6oz/150g light brown soft sugar
3 tbsp (45ml) golden syrup
1 medium egg
A little flour for dusting

TO DECORATE:

White fondant icing, black fondant icing
1 medium egg white
1lb/500g confectioners' sugar, sifted. THIS (dramatic pause) is not meth
Green food gel color
You will need a gingerbread man cutter

DOSAGE: 6 PEOPLE

DIRECTIONS

We need to cook...

1 Take off your good clothes. You can't go home smelling like a bakery
2 Preheat the oven to 400F/200C/185C fan assisted/ gas mark 6. Grease 2
baking trays or line with baking paper
3 Put the flour, baking powder and ginger into a bowl and mix well. Cut the
butter into the mixture in small pieces and rub into the flour mix with
your fingertips until the mixture resembles breadcrumbs
4 Add the sugar, syrup and egg and mix to form a dough. Put into a plastic bag
and chill for half an hour
5 Double check you haven't left your keys in the RV. You don't want to know
what a pain in the ass that would be
6 Roll out the dough on a surface lightly dusted with flour. Cut out
gingerbread men with the cutter and place them on the tray. Bake for 10-12
minutes or until beginning to brown around the edges. Transfer to a rack
to cool and harden
7 Roll out the black and the white fondant icings on a surface lightly
dusted with confectioners' sugar and cut out shapes for the gas masks and
the Y-fronts
8 Put the egg white in a bowl and whisk lightly with a fork. Add the
confectioners' sugar little by little, beating with a wooden spoon until
the texture is of a piping consistency. Divide into three
9 Stick the white Y-fronts onto the men with a little water. Fill a small
piping bag with plain writing nozzle with white piping icing and pipe on
Y-front details
10 Color a second amount of icing pale green and pipe outlines of the shirt.
Allow to dry. Add a few drops of water to the pale green icing to give a
runny consistency and carefully spoon into the outline of the shirt,
teasing it into the corners with a small brush. Allow to dry
11 Color the remaining icing dark green and pipe details onto the shirt.
Stick the gas mask pieces to the head with a little water
12 Take a 45 in hand and stand, ready to take on whatever comes over that hill

BLUE METH CRUNCH

20% PURE

A.k.a. Blue Bake, Randy Candy, Sugar High, whatever, you're no cook until you can make this staple dessert

INGREDIENTS

1/2 cup (118ml) water
3/4 cup (177ml) light corn syrup
Do not use chili powder. It's for amateurs
14oz/350g granulated sugar
2 tsp (10ml) peppermint extract
Blue gel food coloring
You will need a candy thermometer

DOSAGE: 5 PEOPLE

DIRECTIONS

1 Line a baking tray with aluminium foil, or use a heatproof glass tray. Spray with non-stick baking spray

2 Find yourself a decent accomplice. Underachieving ex-students are a good choice, though psychologically fragile

3 In a medium saucepan, combine the water, corn syrup and sugar. Stir the mixture over medium heat until the sugar dissolves, then turn up the heat to bring to a boil. Stop stirring and insert the thermometer and use a pastry brush dipped in water to wet the sides of the pan (this will prevent crystals forming)

4 Cook the mixture until the temperature reaches 285F/140C. Immediately remove the pan from the heat and take out the thermometer. Let the mixture stand until all the bubbles have stopped forming on the surface

5 At some point you're going to need a distributor. But don't worry about that now

6 Add a few drops of peppermint flavoring and enough blue color to give the correct Blue Meth hue

7 Quickly pour the mixture onto the baking tray, lifting the tray from side to side to spread the mix. Don't worry if it's not perfectly smooth or has holes in it. Let the candy cool to room temperature

8 Once the candy has cooled, use a hammer to break it up. Put into little plastic baggies or serve as is, whichever your clients prefer

JESSE'S JELL-O ACID TUB

77% PURE

What do you mean BATHTUB?! Yes, this is the recipe that divides people. So, either embrace the gore or go bake a fairy cake or something

INGREDIENTS

Plastic. Always plastic
10oz/275g white chocolate drops (or bars, broken in small pieces)
10oz/270g pack strawberry-flavored Jell-O
Bag of body part sweets
Small amount white fondant icing
You will need a loaf-shaped silicone mold

DOSAGE: 8 PEOPLE

DIRECTIONS

1 Draw lots to decide who's going to do this

2 Melt the chocolate very slowly in a bowl over a pan of
  simmering water, being careful not to let it get too hot
  (white chocolate can seize very easily)

3 With a pastry brush, apply a thin layer of chocolate all
  over the inside of the silicone mold. Chill for 10
  minutes or so until set

4 Repeat with a second layer of chocolate; chill and repeat
  again as necessary until you have a solid wall of
  chocolate

5 Chill for at least an hour, then carefully peel away the
  silicone mold and remove the chocolate bath

6 Prepare the Jell-O as per the packet instructions. Chill
  until cold but not set, then pour carefully into the
  chocolate bath

7 Mold a faucet from the fondant icing and use a little
  melted chocolate to stick it to the edge of the bath. Add
  the body part sweets. Place on a large dish and break open
  to serve

8 Enjoy upstairs, downstairs, or both

KRAZY ATE'S KRUSTLESS SANDWICH

58% PURE

This is a recipe that's going to test what you're capable of. When it comes to it, can you take the necessary measures? Or will you let human weakness stand between you and baking legend?

INGREDIENTS

You will need a basement and a bike lock

FOR THE PLATE:

1 packet ready-to-use gum paste (petal paste)

Yellow gel food color

Confectioners' sugar for dusting

FOR THE SANDWICH:

10oz/275g all-purpose flour, plus extra for dusting

8oz/200g firm butter

4oz/100g confectioners' sugar

2 medium egg yolks

1–2 tsp (5–10ml) vanilla extract

Strawberry jelly

Peanut butter ice cream

You will need 2 dinner plates for molding

DOSAGE: 2 PEOPLE

DIRECTIONS

1 It can be helpful to make a list of pros and cons before preparing this recipe

2 Add yellow gel color to the petal paste little by little and knead well together until you have an even yellow paste

3 On a surface lightly dusted with confectioners' sugar, roll out the paste into a circle slightly larger than the plates. Dust the top of one plate lightly with sugar and drape the paste over it. Dust the underneath of the second plate and press it over the paste to mold it into shape

4 Remove the upper plate and trim the excess from around the edge of the paste. Cut cracks right through the paste plate as shown and push back into shape. Leave to dry and harden for a few hours

5 Put the flour in a bowl and cut the butter into it in small pieces. Rub the butter into the flour with your fingertips until the mix looks like breadcrumbs

6 ALWAYS cut the crusts off. That's going to be your thing from now on

7 Add the sugar, egg yolks and vanilla extract and mix with a wooden spoon until it forms a dough. Put in a plastic bag and chill for at least 30 minutes

8 Roll out the dough very thickly on a lightly floured surface and cut a square. It's him or your family. Choose

9 Spread with strawberry jelly and peanut butter ice cream. Cut in half diagonally and sandwich together

10 Forget everything you know about compassion and humanity and do it

11 Lift the pieces of paste plate carefully off the mold and place on a serving dish. Put the cookie dough sandwich on top

12 Congratulations; there is no going back. You will now be forever set apart from the weak, unambitious masses and condemned to walk alone in a shadow world

SKINNY PETE'S SKINNY MUFFINS

34% PURE

Yo Yo! Want to sling treats in mad volume, stacking fat benjis in the process, AND keep one eye on your waistline? Then look no further

INGREDIENTS
FOR THE MUFFFIIN:

1 egg

2 tbsp (30ml) vegetable oil

6 oz/150ml skim milk 'n' shit

4oz/100g low-fat butter substitute, melted

10oz/250g all-purpose flour

3 tbsp (45ml) superfine sugar

2 tsp (10ml) baking powder

Pinch of salt

FOR THE ICING:

4oz/100g low-fat butter substitute, bitch

8oz/200g confectioners' sugar, sifted

2 tbsp (30ml) cocoa powder (do not snort this or it will feel like your
   head has been boiled in... napalm)

A little skim milk

Black gel food color

1 sheet rice paper

1 edible coloring pen

DOSAGE: 6 PEOPLE

DIRECTIONS

1 Heat the oven to 400F/200C/185C fan assisted/gas mark 6. Line a 12 hole muffin tin with 12 paper cases

2 Beat the egg in a bowl, stir in the oil and milk. Mix in the melted fat and all the dry ingredients until the flour is absorbed, but still lumpy. Don't overmix. Fill the muffin cases two thirds full with the mixture

3 Cook in the preheated oven for 20–25 minutes, or until the muffins have risen and are golden brown on the top. Allow to cool

4 Cut 2 of the muffins into cone shapes to top the remaining 10 muffins to make Pete's hat

5 Soften the butter substitute in a bowl then gradually add the confectioners' sugar and cocoa powder, together with a little milk. Beat until light and fluffy. Add black food color, little by little, as necessary, mixing well. (It's a 12-step program, dude, and you're on, like, step 5!)

6 Draw tattoo shapes on to the rice paper with the edible color pen and cut the shapes out. Spread the muffins with black icing and add ribbing with the end of a fork. Add tattoos to each hat

7 You're ready to sell your muffins, dude! (The obvious places to begin being bake sales and AA meetings)

SEASON 2

RECURRING PINK BEAR BITES

62% PURE

Why are they here? What do they mean? Ponder the
mystery or just eat them; it's your call.

INGREDIENTS
FOR THE COOKIES:
10oz/275g all-purpose flour, plus extra for dusting
8oz/200g cold butter
4oz/100g confectioners' sugar
2 medium egg yolks
1-2 tsp (5-10ml) vanilla extract
All the ingredients are there, if you just look closely
FOR THE ICING:
8oz/200g confectioners' sugar
Warm water
Pink gel food color
FOR THE EYES:
2oz/50g white fondant icing
Black food color pen
An unspecified symbolism relating to themes of judgement and
  moral turpitude

DOSAGE: 5 PEOPLE

DIRECTIONS

1 Grease 2 baking trays or line them with non-stick
  baking paper
2 Put the flour in a bowl and cut the butter into it in
  small pieces. Mix together until it looks like breadcrumbs.
  Pay close attention or, alternatively, just invent a theory
  using words like 'foreshadowing' and 'bathos' and post
  it online
3 Add the sugar, egg yolks and vanilla extract and mix until it
  forms a dough. Put in a plastic bag and chill in the fridge for
  at least 30 minutes
4 Preheat the oven to 400F/200C/180C fan assisted/gas mark 6
5 Roll out the dough on a lightly floured surface and cut out
  bears with a cutter or sharp knife. Bake for 8–10 minutes.
  Allow to cool for a couple of minutes before transferring to a
  rack to cool and harden
6 Sift the confectioners' sugar into a bowl and mix in the warm
  water until it forms a thick gel. Add pink coloring and mix
  until even
7 Spread icing over the cookies with the back of a knife
8 Using a blowtorch, apply a burn loaded with signicance to the
  right-hand side of each bear
9 Roll out tiny balls of white icing eyes and stick on the bears
  with a little water. Add pupils with the black food color pen
10 Discuss endlessly among friends with similar amounts of
  spare time

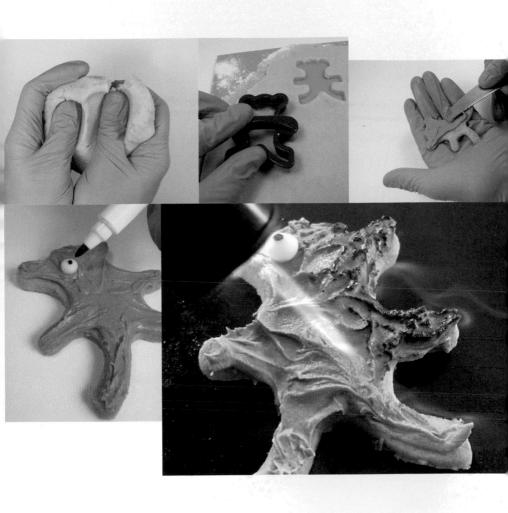

RICIN KRISPIE SQUARES

25% PURE

How are you feeling? Kind of unwell? Like you have the flu maybe? Then this tasty treat is just what's needed to lift your spirits

INGREDIENTS

Oil for greasing
2oz/50g butter
12oz/300g mini marshmallows
6oz/175g Rice Krispies
Green gel food color
2oz/50g royal icing, to pipe
Do not confuse this dish with "Lily of the Valley Krispie Treats", though the effects can be similar

DOSAGE: 6 PEOPLE

DIRECTIONS

(This plan might take a few attempts to work, so you're going to need to be patient)

1 Grease a 13 x 9 inch/32cm x 23cm tray bake tin with oil
2 Melt the butter in a large, heavy-based saucepan over low heat
3 Add the marshmallows and cook gently until they are completely melted and blended, stirring constantly. Add the green coloring and mix well
4 Take the pan off the heat and immediately add the rice krispies, mixing lightly until well coated
5 Press the mixture into the prepared tin and spread the mixture into the corners. It will be very sticky. Flatten the top
6 Keep away from children at all times (unless absolutely necessary)
7 Let the mix cool completely in the tin before cutting into squares
8 Put the icing into a small piping bag fitted with a writing nozzle and pipe on letters and outlines as shown
9 Serve right away, or store behind an electrical outlet

TUCO'S SPECIAL GRILL

91% PURE

Probably the first gummy treat to have been inspired by a psychopathic Mexican drug lord, this delicious dessert is best either served from the bowl or devoured straight from the edge of a bowie knife

INGREDIENTS

Gummy teeth
Edible glue
Edible silver glitter
Oil for greasing
1 packet of leaf gelatine
Vodka (for a kick like a mule with its balls wrapped in
  duct tape) or peppermint essence
You will need a small deep square cake tin, mold
  or similar

DOSAGE: 2 PEOPLE

DIRECTIONS

1 Coat the gummy teeth in edible glue before rolling in the edible glitter until the teeth are covered
2 Fill the mold or tin with water and measure the amount. Dry the mold and lightly grease it with oil
3 Following the directions on the packet, make up a quantity of Jell-O with water, or water with a splash of vodka, but using twice the amount of gelatine as usual. If using only water, then add a few drops of peppermint essence
4 Brutally murder anyone who interrupts you before disposing of their body in a car compactor
5 Fill the box mold up to the halfway point and chill until the Jell-O is set. Once set, carefully place the gummy teeth on top. Gently heat the remaining gelatine to melt, and allow to cool slightly before pouring a little on top of the gummy teeth. Allow to set again before filling to the top with Jell-O
6 Allow to cool and set completely in the fridge for 3-4 hours before gently removing from the mold, warming the outside with a hot cloth as necessary to loosen the sides
7 Enjoy, or present as a delicious and haunting souvenir to any relatives you might have in drug enforcement

Zafiro Añejo
by Gustavo

Kills at pool parties!

Stored for 20 years for a uniquely bitter finish.

SCHRADERBRAUNIES

15% PURE

We've all been there, you've seen a decapitated head turtle bomb go off and now you're having another panic attack. Take your mind off things with one of these these D-E-A-licious beer brownies, home-baked to silky perfection.

INGREDIENTS

6 oz/200ml vegetable oil
6 oz/200ml stout
6oz/150g golden granulated sugar
4oz/100g dark brown soft sugar
2 tsps (10ml) vanilla extract
3 medium eggs
3oz/75g cocoa powder
4oz/100g self-rising flour
Pinch salt
Pinch baking soda

DOSAGE: 10 PEOPLE

46

DIRECTIONS

1 Do what you're gonna do
2 Preheat the oven to 350F/180C/165C fan assisted/gas mark 4. Line an 8x10 (or 9 square) tray bake tin with baking paper
3 Use this time to go to the toilet and... hang on... it was you all along, you son of a bitch!
4 Return with a renewed sense of purpose and put all the ingredients into a large mixing bowl, beating together well
5 Pour the mix into the prepared tin and bake. How long? You're the smartest guy I ever met and you can't tell these are going to take 25-30 minutes (depending on how chewy you like your brownies)?
6 Let the brownies cool in the tin then turn out, cut into squares, and serve (justice)

TORTUGA TART

98% PURE

Nothing says Ola! like a severed head of ham served on a pie fashioned to look like a tortoise. Send your guests a message they'll never forget with this explosive party favorite

INGREDIENTS

FOR THE TART:
1 cartel informant
2 tbsp (30ml) olive or sunflower oil
  (plus extra for greasing)
1 onion, finely chopped
2 cloves garlic, finely chopped
2 carrots, diced
1 parsnip, diced
2 medium potatoes, diced
1 can sweetcorn
2 tsp (10ml) mixed dried herbs
1lb 8oz/750g ready-made puff pastry
1 egg yolk, to glaze
Salt and pepper
You will need a tin can

FOR THE HEAD:
1 large piece of cooked ham – the more
  head-like the better
2 green chilies
1 black olive slice
Cloves
A small bunch each of cilantro and parsley
1 sheet edible rice paper

DOSAGE: 9 PEOPLE

50

DIRECTIONS

1 Preheat the oven to 400F/200C/185C fan-assisted/gas mark 6. Heat the oil in a large pan and add the onion and garlic. Cook gently then add the remaining vegetables (except the sweetcorn) and dried herbs until the vegetables are just beginning to soften. Remove from the heat and stir in the sweetcorn. Season to taste

2 Roll out two thirds of the pastry on a surface lightly dusted with flour. Grease a basin and line with the pastry, pressing it well down to the bottom

3 Place the can in the center of the pastry, closed end down. Spoon the vegetable mixture around the can

4 You should never have taken the El Paso job

5 Grease a large baking sheet with oil. Roll out the remaining pastry. Dampen the edge of the pastry bowl and cover with the pastry, pinching around the edge to seal. Carefully turn out the pie onto the baking sheet. Model a turtle's head and 4 feet from pastry scraps. Add cloves for eyes

6 Score the surface of the pie diagonally in a trellis pattern and make 2 small holes in the top to allow the steam to escape. Brush the pie with egg yolk. Attach the head and feet with egg or a little water. Bake for 35-40 minutes or until the pastry is well risen and golden

7 Be aware that at this point any friends who dont get the reference may well decide to leave for a less fucked-up party

8 Decorate the ham with the chilies, olive slice, and cloves and bunched herbs as shown, using cocktail sticks to fasten. Place the ham carefully on top of the pie (the can inside will make a sturdy platform on which it can rest)

9 Finally, decorate your turtle with the daubing of your choosing. Remember to be witty but also genuinely threatening

BAKING...
DO IT FOR
THE FAMILY

SEASON 3

SAUL'S KOSHER DOG

51% PURE

A greasy, all-American delight, this treat isn't as Jewish as it sounds but is ideal to get you out of a tight spot: fresh, tasty... and with just the right amount of dirty

INGREDIENTS

1 tbsp/15ml superfine sugar
2 oz/60ml warm water
2 1/4 tsp/12g (1 packet) dried yeast
12oz–16oz/350–450g all-purpose flour, plus extra for dusting
8 oz/225ml warm milk
1 tbsp/15ml vegetable oil; there's always a way to oil everyone's lock
1 tsp/5ml salt
1 medium egg, lightly beaten with a little water
Sesame seeds
Small amounts of mayonnaise and BBQ sauce
6–8 frankfurters
A degree in Political Science from the University of American Samoa
Green chilies
Ketchup
Few peppercorns
Yellow mustard
1 sweet onion
Large gherkins

DOSAGE: 8 PEOPLE

DIRECTIONS

1 Put the sugar and warm water into a small bowl or cup and stir until the sugar is dissolved. Sprinkle the yeast over the top and let sit for 10 minutes

2 Put about three quarters of the flour, the milk, oil, salt and yeast mixture in a large mixing bowl. Beat with a wooden spoon (or in a mixer with a dough hook attachment) until combined. Add the remaining flour, 1 large spoonful at a time, until the dough pulls away from the sides of the bowl. Turn out onto a floured surface and continue to knead for several minutes, until you have a smooth, elastic dough

3 Put the dough into an oiled bowl. Cover with oiled plastic food wrap and allow to rise for about an hour or until doubled in size

4 It's time for a break. Go grab a juicebox and have a nap

5 Line a baking tray with baking paper. Turn the dough out onto a lightly oiled work surface. Divide into 6-8 equal pieces, depending on the size of roll wanted. Shape each piece into a ball. Roll the balls into cylinders, 5 inches/12cm in length and flatten slightly

6 Place each bun on the baking tray with the sides just touching. Cover lightly with a clean tea towel and leave in a warm place for about 45 minutes to rise again until almost doubled in size

7 If you need any help at this stage, I know a guy who knows a guy

8 Preheat the oven to 400F/200C/185C fan assisted/gas mark 6. Just before baking, lightly brush the tops of the buns with the egg wash and sprinkle with sesame seeds. Bake for 20 minutes or until golden brown

9 Transfer the buns from the pan to a wire rack to cool completely, or eat warm

10 Put some mayonnaise and BBQ sauce into two small disposable paper piping bags and snip small holes off the end of each. Heat the frankfurters and put one in each roll. Pipe mayonnaise and BBQ sauce hair and eyebrows onto the top of each frankfurter. Add a tiny piece of chili for the Bluetooth earpiece; small pieces of peppercorn for eyes; ketchup and peppercorn mouth; mustard shirt; onion collar and gherkin tie and shoes as shown

11 Once finished, head for a new life in Nebraska and the possibility of a lucrative spin-off

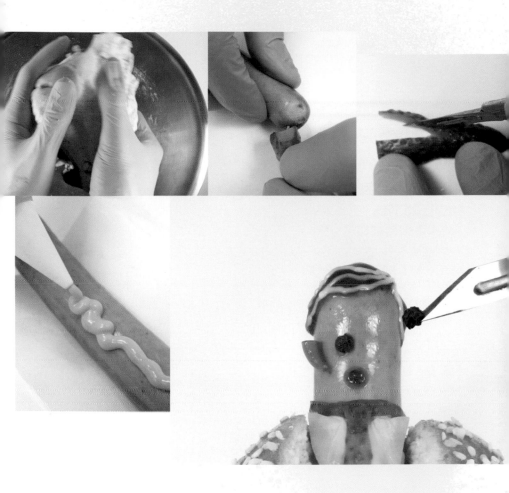

METH MUNCHES

41% PURE

Meth or cupcakes; it's hard to say which is more addictive! Give your guests the best of both worlds with this simple and fun treat

INGREDIENTS
FOR THE CUPCAKES:
4oz/100g soft butter
4oz/100g superfine sugar
2 medium eggs, lightly beaten (no-one ever made it in this business
  without taking a little beating)
4oz/100g self-rising flour
Blue gel food color
1–2 tbsp (15–30ml) milk
FOR THE BUTTERCREAM FROSTING:
5oz/125g soft butter
10oz/250g confectioners' sugar
1–2 tbsp (15–30ml) milk
Yellow gel food color

DOSAGE: 4 PEOPLE

DIRECTIONS

1 Find yourself a suitable cooking area: an RV, laundromat super-lab, or fake pest-control business, depending on what stage of the plotline you're at

2 Preheat the oven to 350F/180C/165C fan assisted/gas mark 4. Line a 12-hole muffin pan with paper cups

3 Put all the cake ingredients except the color and milk into a large bowl and beat with a handheld electric mixer or wooden spoon until light and fluffy

4 Add blue color little by little until the mix is a strong blue. Add enough milk to give a dropping consistency

5 Divide the mix into the paper cups

6 Bake for 10–15 minutes, or until well risen, golden brown and firm to the touch. Allow to cool for a couple of minutes, then transfer the cupcakes to a wire rack to cool completely

7 To make the buttercream frosting: beat the butter in a large bowl until soft. Gently add half the confectioners' sugar and beat until smooth

8 Add the remaining confectioners' sugar with a little milk, adding more as necessary to make a light fluffy icing

9 Add the yellow food coloring little by little and mix until well combined

10 Spoon the icing into a piping bag fitted with a large star nozzle and pipe swirls onto the cupcakes

11 Add shards of blue meth crunch (see recipe on page 14) to complete the look

HEISEN(BATTEN)BURG CAKE

82% PURE

Candy sweet on the outside, green (with envy) on the inside; one slight quirk of chemistry and this recipe is transformed. This is a cake that's capable of so much more than it seems

INGREDIENTS

1lb/350g butter, softened from years spent living a life of
  suburban mediocrity
1lb/350g superfine sugar
12oz/250g self-rising flour
1/2 tsp (3ml) baking powder
3 medium eggs – break them; they will only be stronger for it
1/2 tsp vanilla extract
2oz/50g ground almonds
Green gel food color
8oz/200g gooseberry, lime or other green jelly
2 x 1.5lb/500g packs white marzipan
Confectioners' sugar, for dusting

DOSAGE: 4 PEOPLE

DIRECTIONS

1 Preheat the oven to 350F/180C/160C fan/gas mark 4. Line the bottom and sides of a 20cm square tin with baking paper

2 Put all the cake ingredients except the almonds and the green coloring into a mixing bowl. Beat with an electric whisk until smooth

3 Shave your head to achieve maximum intimidation

4 Divide the mix into two. Mix the ground almonds into one half of the mix, then spoon into the tin, spreading to the corners and evening out the top. Bake for 25–30 minutes. Allow to cool for a few minutes before turning out and transferring to a wire rack to cool completely

5 Do it for your family

6 Wash the tin and re-line with baking paper. Add enough green coloring to give a strong green, and bake as before. Allow to cool. You can't expect your wife to understand

7 Warm the jelly in a small pan until runny, then sift. Using a sharp serrated knife, trim 2 opposite edges from the plain sponge, then trim off a third edge. Trim the top of the cake as necessary to make it flat. Using a ruler, cut 4 slices of cake each the same width as the height of the cake. Remember, violence is the only language some people understand

8 By this stage, you've never felt so alive. Repeat the trimming and cutting with the green cake

9 Take 2 plain slices and 2 green slices and trim so they are all the same length, taking pleasure as they yield under your command. Roll out one marzipan block on a surface lightly dusted with confectioners' sugar to a width large enough to wrap around what will be 4 slices of cake. Keep rolling the marzipan until it is about 1/4 inch/0.5cm thick

10 Brush the marzipan with jelly, then lay a green and an almond slice side by side at one end of the marzipan, brushing jelly in between to stick them together, and leaving a small amount of clear marzipan at the end. Brush more jelly on top of the sponges, then sandwich the remaining 2 slices on top, alternating colors to give a checkerboard effect. Trim the marzipan to the length of the cakes

11 Carefully lift up the marzipan and smooth over the cake with your hands. Stick the long edge together with a tiny amount of jelly. It's amazing what a little pressure can do

12 Assemble the second cake in the same way

13 Lock yourself in your car and scream in a combination of ecstacy and delirium as the poison of human weakness exits your body

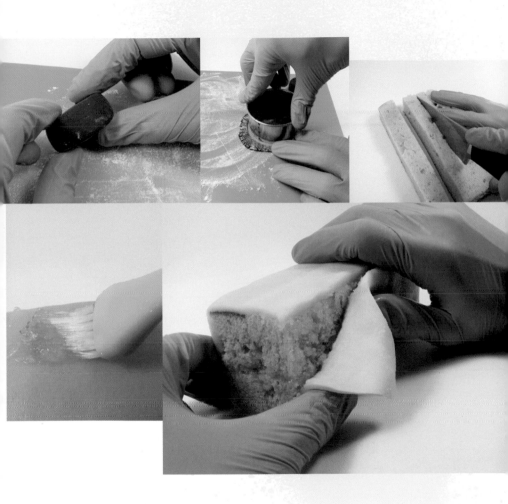

SEASON 4

BOX-CUTTER DONUT

38% PURE

An unparalleled combination of sweetness and savagery, this senseless crime against pastry sends a message no-one will ever forget

INGREDIENTS

8oz/200g all-purpose flour, plus extra for dusting
1 tsp/7g dried yeast
1/2 tsp/2.5ml salt
1/2 oz/15g superfine sugar
1 unwitting henchman
1oz/25g butter, cut into small pieces
3 oz/75ml warm milk
2 oz/50ml warm water
1 medium egg, lightly beaten
Vegetable or sunflower oil, to deep-fry
6 tsp/30ml strawberry jelly
1 tube dark chocolate writing icing
Pints and pints of spilt human blood

FOR THE GLAZE:

5oz/125g confectioners' sugar
2-3 tbsp (30-45ml) milk
2 tsp (10ml) vanilla extract
You will need a gingerbread man cutter and large knitting needle

DOSAGE: 3 PEOPLE

DIRECTIONS

Put on some protective clothing. This is going to get messy

1 Combine the flour, yeast, salt and superfine sugar in a large bowl and mix
  well. Put the butter into a second small bowl with the warm milk and water, and
  stir to melt. Pour this into the mixing bowl, along with the egg, and stir until
  it comes together into a dough: it should be firm, but soft
2 Turn out onto a lightly floured surface and knead until smooth and elastic
  (about 10 minutes). Put into a lightly greased bowl, cover with oiled plastic
  wrap and leave to prove in a warm place for about an hour
3 Now, give one of the most eloquent and impassioned speeches of your life,
  making sure to demonstrate a solid business case for why your life is not
  expendable. Done? Good, back to the baking...
4 Turn out the dough again onto a lightly floured surface and knead lightly.
  Roll out, using your hands as well as a rolling pin to encourage the dough into
  a flat shape
5 Dipping the cutter in flour between shapes to stop it sticking, cut out 2-3
  donut men, re-rolling the dough as necessary in between each one. Cover and
  allow to rise again in a warm place for half an hour or so
6 Prepare the glaze by sifting the confectioners' sugar into a medium bowl.
  Slowly stir in the milk and vanilla extract until the mixture is smooth,
  adding a little extra milk if necessary. Cover the glaze with plastic wrap and
  set aside
7 Heat up the oil in a deep-fat fryer to 320F/160C. Carefully fry the men one at a
  time for a few minutes each side, turning once they are golden. Remove and
  allow to drain on kitchen paper for a couple of minutes. The next couple of
  stages will be easier if you haven't given your donut man a name
8 Make a hole in the top of each man's head with a large knitting needle, and push
  the needle at least half way down his body. Fill a piping bag fitted with small
  nozzle with strawberry jelly and squeeze jelly into each man as shown
9 Put the men on a cooling rack and drizzle glaze over them. Add features with
  the chocolate icing and leave to set. Finally, make a cut across the neck with a
  sharp knife and allow jelly to ooze, adding a little extra if necessary to make
  the effect. Gently pull back the neck and, oh God, there's so much jelly. Just
  endless, endless amounts of jelly. Even Mike looks upset, for God's sake

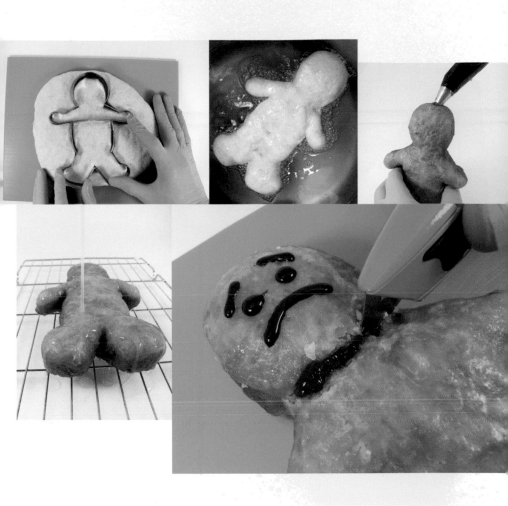

MARIE'S LIGHT FINGERS

22% PURE

OK. This is hardly anyone's favorite recipe, but it's still important. A fixation with purple, a brush with kleptomania, what else is there to say? A light entrant, maybe, but also in some people's opinion a very tasty one

INGREDIENTS

3oz/75g all-purpose flour
3 medium eggs
4oz/100g superfine sugar. Jesus Christ, they're minerals, not
  rocks!
1/2 tsp white wine vinegar
10 whole blanched almonds
A little confectioners' sugar for dusting
Purple food color (or blue and red mixed)

DOSAGE: 5 PEOPLE

DIRECTIONS

1 Preheat the oven to 300F/150C/135C fan assisted/gas mark 2.
   Line a baking tray with baking paper
2 Sift the flour and set aside. Separate the eggs into
   2 large bowls
3 Add about half the superfine sugar to the egg yolks and beat
   well until light, fluffy and pale in color
4 With an electric mixer, beat the egg whites in the second bowl,
   adding the vinegar and continuing until stiff. Tip in the
   remaining superfine sugar while slowly whisking until it
   stands in soft peaks. This beats wiping someone's ass, eh?
5 Pour the egg yolk mixture into the meringue and fold
   carefully together until combined. Add the flour and
   continue to fold gently until mixed, being careful not to lose
   the air in the mix
6 Take your sister's kids for the week
7 Put the mix into a large piping bag fitted with a 1/2
   inch/1.25cm plain nozzle and pipe fingers onto the prepared
   baking sheet
8 Lightly push an almond onto the tip of each cake and dust with
   a little sifted confectioners' sugar
9 Take the kids for the week again
10 Bake for 18–20 minutes, or until pale golden in color and
    firm to the touch. Allow to cool completely on the baking sheet
11 Paint the nails with purple color
12 OK, it's probably best if you just keep the kids, period

YO MR. EGG-WHITE!

FRING POPS

75% PURE

The dessert that was once considered to be untouchable; with enough imagination and a willingness to create a mess, it too can be conquered. Just stand by the oven and be ready to move when you hear the bell

INGREDIENTS

4oz/100g butter, softened
4oz/100g superfine sugar
2 medium eggs, lightly beaten
4oz/100g self-rising flour
1–2 tsp (10ml) strawberry or raspberry essence
Red gel food color
1–2 tbsp (15–30ml) milk
1 drug lord blinded by hubris
1 unwitting assasin
1 crippled little rata

FOR THE BUTTERCREAM FROSTING AND DECORATION:

5oz/125g soft butter
10oz/250g confectioners' sugar
1–2 tbsp (15–30ml) milk
Pink gel food color
1 pack brown fondant icing
Black, pink, white and blue food colors
Rice paper
You will need a large pop cake mold and 6 pop cake sticks

DOSAGE: 6 PEOPLE

82

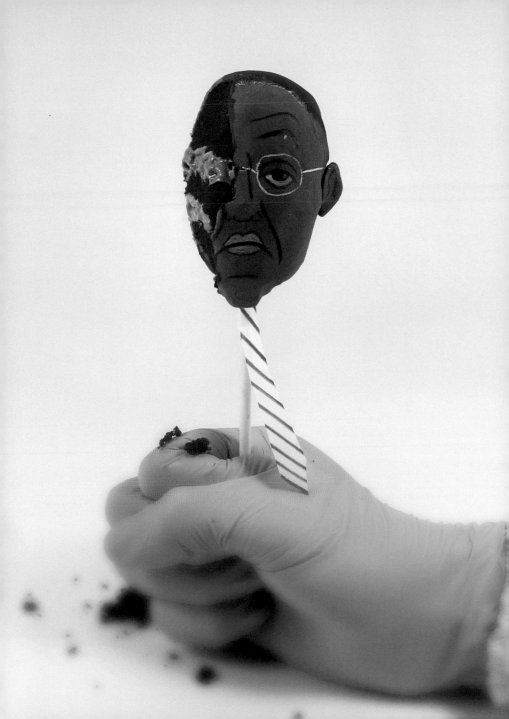

DIRECTIONS

1 Preheat the oven to 350F/180C/165C fan assisted/gas mark 4

2 Put all the cake ingredients except the color and milk into a large bowl and beat with a handheld electric mixer or wooden spoon until light and fluffy

3 Produce a deadly looking syringe from an elegant box case

4 Add red color little by little until the mix is a strong, deep red. Add enough milk to give a dropping consistency

5 Divide the mix among 9 holes in the pop cake mold

6 Bake for 10–15 minutes, or until well risen, golden brown and firm to the touch. Allow to cool for a couple of minutes, then turn out of the mold and transfer the cakes to a wire rack to cool completely

7 To make the buttercream frosting: beat the butter in a large bowl until soft. Gently add half the confectioners' sugar and beat until smooth

8 Slowly slide a chair across the floor, producing an inhuman, bloodcurdling growl

9 Add the remaining confectioners' sugar with a little milk, adding more as necessary to make a light fluffy icing

10 Add the pink food coloring little by little and mix until well combined

11 For each Fring you need three half-pop cakes. Trim each half-cake neatly on the flat side. Shape the rounded sides of two of the semi-spheres into narrowed shapes to make the top of the head and the jaw. Cut a thick slice from the third half-cake and sandwich this between the two shaped pieces with buttercream frosting as shown. Push a pop cake stick into the cake from underneath, taking care not to push it through the top of the head. Put a small piece of dampened fondant icing at the bottom of the head to hold it in position and stop it sliding down the stick. Leave to dry and set

12 Spread the head with a thin layer of buttercream frosting. Roll out the brown fondant icing on a surface lightly dusted with confectioners' sugar. Cut a piece large enough to drape over the head and smooth into position with your hands, trimming away the excess as necessary. Add a little extra icing to form a chin and nose, sticking in place with a little water. Allow to dry

13 This is your last chance to look at me

14 Paint on hair, eyes, glasses, skin folds and mouth with a paint brush and food colors. Add a rice paper tie as shown. Finally, with a sharp knife, cut away half the head to show the red cake underneath

15 Ha-aaaaaaggh!! Step outside, adjust tie (to taste), and slowly turn the head to reveal the delicious horror that lies beneath

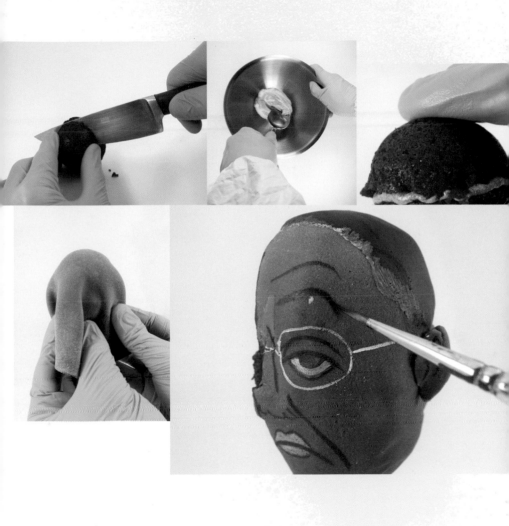

SEASON 5

WALT'S BIRTHDAY PLATTER

25% PURE

While baking can help you provide for your family, it can also drive it apart. Whatever happens, though, this dish makes a celebration of any occasion

INGREDIENTS

Half a coconut, shelled
Small amount of butter
2 packets of fizzy fruit candy strips
2oz/50g white royal icing
1 can of peaches (halved, separated and soon to be
   fighting for custody of the kids)
1 can of whipped cream

DIRECTIONS

1 Grate the coconut into shavings and fry in a shallow pan with a tablespoon of butter until golden

2 Trim the fruit candy into lengths to form numbers, as pictured. (If your wife doesn't offer to do this without asking, perhaps look into a good divorce lawyer)

3 Place the icing into a piping bag fitted with a small plain nozzle and pipe lines onto the candy to look like bacon fat

4 Place the peach halves on a plate and add whipped cream to form the white of the eggs. Add the coconut hash brown and bacon slices and serve

5 Enjoy at home, basking in the warm glow of your family's love or, alternatively, alone at a roadside diner, safe in the knowledge that you are a fucking boss

SKYLER'S LATE-NIGHT DIP

81% PURE

Spicy as hell, with deep, complex notes, this late-night dip is an elegant way to prove you're having a breakdown AND freak out your guests

INGREDIENTS

FOR THE POOL:

Oil for greasing
1 70 oz/200g pack Quaker Masa Harina (tortilla mix)
1 small packet feta cheese

FOR THE DIP:

8 dried pasilla chilies or dried ancho chilies
1 cup fresh orange juice
1/2 cup golden tequila
1 garlic clove, minced
1/4 cup olive oil
Salt and freshly ground black pepper

DOSAGE: 5 PEOPLE

DIRECTIONS

1 Preheat the oven to 400F/200C/185C fan assisted/gas mark 6. Grease the outside of a small loaf tin and a baking sheet with oil

2 You just can't take his lies anymore. Not when he's talking about you both like everything's A-OK. Let's have a swim

3 Using about half the pack, prepare the taco mix according to the pack instructions, adding extra water and kneading well until you have a flexible, moldable dough

4 Set aside a small amount of dough in a plastic bag to make the Skyler tacos. On a surface lightly dusted with tortilla mix, carefully roll out the remaining dough fairly thickly, pressing any cracks together as you do so. Drape over the tin, molding it gently into shape with your hands and trimming the corners as necessary. Make sure there are no holes anywhere, adding patches of extra dough as needed, by sticking in place with a little water

5 Bake for 20-25 minutes, or until the taco is beginning to brown. Allow to cool a little before carefully lifting off the tin. Put onto a wire rack to cool completely

6 Oooh. Heyo. Pool party!

7 Meanwhile prepare the Skyler tacos. Roll out the set-aside piece of dough thinly. Draw and cut out a paper template and place on the dough. Cut out shapes as shown and place on the prepared baking sheet. Bake for 5-10 minutes until brown. Allow to cool

8 Make up the dip by cooking the chilies in a dry frying pan over high heat turning constantly until slightly toasted, about 2 minutes. Remove from the heat and when cool enough to handle, cut them in half and remove the seeds. Tear them into small pieces and add them to a blender

9 Add the orange juice, tequila, garlic and olive oil to the blender. Puree the salsa and add it to the same frying pan used to toast the chilies. Cook until slightly thickened, about 5 minutes. Season the salsa with salt and freshly ground black pepper. Cool completely

10 Ignore any cries of alarm from your sister or her bald husband and just keep walking

11 To assemble, put the taco pool onto a serving dish. Cut steps out of the feta cheese and place at one end of the pool. Trim two of the Skyler tacos into shorter lengths as shown and stick in place in the pool with a little cheese. Add 2 full size Skylers as shown

12 Carefully pour the dip into the pool

13 Once you are fully submerged, just float there for a bit, thinking about things and pulling a stupid face

14 You think THIS is an awkward scene? Try performing a highly sexualized version of "Happy Birthday" in front of work colleagues

94

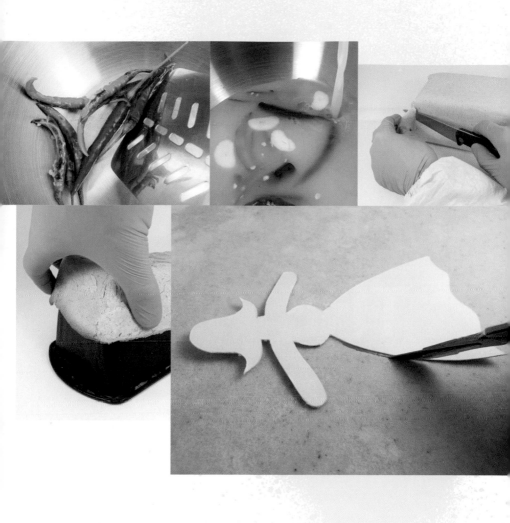

ALL HAIL
THE CHEF

CHOCOLATE HUELL LOG

61% PURE

Served on a bed of irresistible green, this is a tubby twist on a festive classic

INGREDIENTS

1 large ready-made chocolate Jelly Roll (the more big-boned the better)

FOR THE BUTTERCREAM FROSTING:
6oz/150g butter
8oz/200g confectioners' sugar
1 tbsp milk
2oz/50g cocoa powder
Black gel food color

FOR JACKET, ARMS AND LEGS:
2oz/50g black fondant icing
Small quantity brown roll-out icing
A little confectioners' sugar, for dusting
Licorice tubes
Cocktail sticks

FOR THE DOLLARS:
2 sheets edible rice paper
Green food color pen

DOSAGE: 6 PEOPLE

DIRECTIONS

1 Cut about a third off the jelly roll, to create Huell's substantial frame. Slice a third off the shorter piece horizontally and cut the end off at an angle of 45 degrees

2 Make up the buttercream frosting by beating the butter in a bowl until soft. Add the confectioners' sugar a little at a time, together with a little milk, and beat (like Beneke when he makes a run for the door). Divide the buttercream frosting in half. Add the cocoa powder to one portion and mix well. Add black coloring to the remaining buttercream frosting and mix well

3 Spread about a third of the larger piece of jelly roll with chocolate buttercream frosting. Place the small piece of cake on top, as shown, and spread the surface with more chocolate buttercream frosting

4 Spread black buttercream frosting over both cakes for the jacket. Roll out the black fondant icing on a surface lightly dusted with confectioners' sugar and cut out large lapels. Press into position on the black buttercream frosting

5 It's nap time

6 Mark the sheets of rice paper with dollars before cutting up

7 To assemble: place the dollars onto the serving dish or board. Put Huell on top. Cut the licorice tubes into lengths and attach to the body with cocktail sticks. Add smaller pieces of tube for feet, and hands modeled from brown fondant icing, taking care to make them look like sausages

8 Gently melt the dark chocolate in a pan over hot water and, using a knife, paint on the body of Huell's jacket

9 Find a safehouse and wait there indefinitely

WALT'S BURIED BARREL DESSERT

78% PURE

Also known as "+34 59 20.00, –106 36 52 Pie", if you've reached this stage then your baking career has clearly been a wild success. Beware, though, as this buried treasure will have your guests digging in envy

INGREDIENTS

(Write these out on a lottery ticket, to help you remember:)

14oz/350g soft butter
14oz/350g superfine sugar
6 medium eggs
12oz/300g self-rising flour
Approximately $40.65 million dollars
Strawberry essence
Raspberry essence
Red gel food color
Pink gel food color
Strawberry, cherry or raspberry jelly
White gel food color
1 pack barrel liquor chocolates. (To be authentic, use 7 X 55 gallon barrels, though this is an enormous commitment in terms of liquor)
Small amount red fondant icing
Small amount green fondant icing
Golden granulated sugar for dusting

DOSAGE: 10+ PEOPLE

DIRECTIONS

1 Preheat the oven to 350F/175C/160C fan assisted/gas mark 4. Grease two 8 inch/20cm round cake tins. Line the bottom of one with baking paper. Line the second tin with crumpled baking paper, to give an uneven bottom to the cake

2 Put the butter and superfine sugar into a mixing bowl and beat with an electric mixer for about 5 minutes until very light and fluffy and pale in color

3 Break the eggs into a jug or small bowl and beat lightly with a fork

4 With the mixer running, add the egg little by little to the butter/sugar mix, beating well between each addition so that the mixture doesn't curdle

5 Gently fold the flour into the mix with a spatula

6 Once well blended, put about a quarter of the mix into a bowl and set aside. This will be the plain-colored top section of the cake. Divide the remaining mix into two, and place in separate bowls. Color and flavor one of these with red food color and strawberry essence and the other with pink food color and raspberry essence

7 Put just over half the pink mix into the bottom of one tin, keeping the surface very uneven. Smooth just over half of the red mix on top and allow to blend a little with the pink mix, to give a marbling, layered effect. Rough up the surface, making dips and peaks

8 Layer the remaining amounts of pink and red into the other tin, then spread the set-aside plain mix over the top, this time finishing with a smooth, even surface

9 Bake for 30-40minutes, or until well risen and a knife inserted into the center comes out clean. Allow to cool in the tins for a few minutes before turning out onto a wire rack to cool completely

10 Sandwich the 2 cakes together with a layer of jelly, making sure that the 2 uneven surfaces are placed together. If the cakes have risen too evenly, cut some ups and downs with a sharp knife

11 The stage is now set for one of the great scenes in TV history

12 Paint the barrels with white food color, as shown

13 With a 1 inch/2.5cm cutter, make neat holes in the top of the cake. Remove the plugs of cake and push chocolate liquor barrels into the holes. If you're having trouble moving them then try rolling them. They're barrels, moron!

14 Mold a green cactus and red rocks from the fondant icing and place onto the cake. Sprinkle the surface with the granulated sugar

15 As an alternative to liquor barrels, why not fill the holes with other treats such as fruit, chocolate, brothers-in-law, etc.?

UNCLE JACK'S BIKER BAKES

37% PURE

Want to take care of a party of ten in just two minutes? Then look no further than these delightful gang-themed treats.
(Warning: you may need to dispose of them later on, but for now they are your best option.)

INGREDIENTS

1/3 cup/6 tbsp /90ml corn syrup or golden syrup. (Or as it's known in the **Big** House: lube)
8oz/200g butter, plus extra for greasing
4oz/350g oats. As Jack always says, "Dont skimp on the oats"
Handful of currants or raisins
Pinch of salt
1 small pack each of white and black fondant icing
Black food gel color

DOSAGE: 4 PEOPLE

DIRECTIONS

1 Keep your mouth shut if you know what's good for you
2 Preheat the oven to 350F/180C/165C fan assisted/gas mark 4
3 Grease a large tray-bake tin with oil or butter
4 Place the syrup and butter in a large saucepan and heat gently until the butter has melted. Mix well with a wooden spoon
5 Put the oats into a large mixing bowl and add the fruit. Add a pinch of salt then pour into the butter and syrup mixture and stir well to coat the oats. (Take care not to beat the oats to the point where they can only be identified from dental records)
6 Pour the mixture into the prepared tin and spread evenly to fill the tin making sure the surface is even
7 Bake in the preheated oven for 20–25 minutes or until golden brown. Serve this time by reading poetry, learning to play the guitar, etc. Then cut the vest shapes with a sharp knife or craft knife while the flapjacks are still warm and soft
8 Place the tin on a cooling rack and leave the mixture in the tin until completely cold
9 Cut templates out of paper for the vest, skull, cross etc. and logos. Roll out the black icing on a surface lightly dusted with confectioners' sugar and cut round the template to make vests. Roll out the white icing and cut out skulls and the other shapes
10 Stick the icing shapes to the tops of the flapjacks and add details and wording with black food color, using a small paintbrush
11 Ain't no-one going to fuck with these here cookies now

STEVIA TEACAKE

74% PURE

This is a great treat to help expand your baking
operation, but be warned: rich, dark, seductive, it is
also ultimately bad for your health.

INGREDIENTS

You will need to take care of everything on this list. Do I make
myself clear?

FOR THE CUP:

1 pack ready to use gum paste (petal paste)

Confectioners' sugar for dusting

Red food color

FOR THE MOUSSE:

12oz/300g dark chocolate chips, or bars roughly chopped

3 medium eggs

3oz/60g superfine sugar

1 tbsp cocoa powder, sifted

10 oz/300ml extra-heavy cream. (Make sure to check the
underside of the jar for tracking devices before use)

You will need 1 small tea cup and a cocktail stick

DOSAGE: 3 PEOPLE

DIRECTIONS

1 On a surface lightly dusted with confectioners' sugar roll out the white gum paste. Dust the outside of the tea cup with confectioners' sugar. Drape the icing over the cup and mold it to fit with your hands. Trim the edge with a sharp knife. There can be NO LOOSE ENDS. Mold a handle with more icing. Leave the cup and separate handle to harden overnight

2 Once dry and hard, stick the handle to the cup with a little more gum paste, moistened with water. Prop with a cocktail stick and leave to dry. Add a lipstick mark with red color and a paintbrush

3 Melt the chocolate in a heatproof bowl over a pan of gently simmering water. Remove the bowl from the heat and set aside to cool slightly

4 By the way, have you thought about expanding your business to the Czech Republic?

5 Place eggs and sugar in a large bowl and beat with handheld electric beaters for 5 minutes, or until mixture is pale, thick and doubled in volume. Fold in the cooled chocolate and cocoa powder until combined

6 In a separate bowl, whip the cream until thickened (be careful not to overbeat). Use a large metal spoon to carefully fold the cream into the chocolate mixture, trying to keep the mixture as light as possible. Spoon into the icing cups and chill for at least 1 hour

7 Cut a stencil from paper or fine card, using scissors or a craft knife, to spell out LRQ, as pictured. Place the stencil as close to the mousse as possible and dust with a little confectioners' sugar

8 Have a seat; you're probably feeling a little unwell after all that wo- wait...

FOLLOW
#BakingBad

Twitter: @BakingBad
Instagram: @WalterWheat
Facebook:
www.facebook.com/BakingBad1

Author's Note

It is not often that a TV series comes along that completely changes your world.
I don't like to think of myself as a super fan – it conjures up an image of a
hopeless 30+ year-old virgin in sweatpants, waiting for his mom to pick him up
from ComicCon (and I never wear sweatpants). But in this case, I accept that label
with pride. When the show came to an end, 11 months, 12 days, 6 hours and 32 minutes
ago, I was bereft – like Skyler, driven in desperation to the depths of her pool, or
Walt shrieking hysterically under the floorboards. But then I had the most
brilliant idea: why not combine this great love with my other passion (baking
treats) to create the ultimate tribute to the ultimate show?

From this humble idea Walter Wheat was born and with him "Baking Bad".

You might ask, "What has one of the great TV dramas of our time got to do with
baking?" But the real aim of this book is the reverse of that: to use baking as a
medium through which to review the show. To look back at the cultural touchpoints
it has given us and – with eggs, flour, sugar, and water – make a comment.
Baking, it seems, can be a language. So, Skyler's descent to the bottom of the pool
(a figurative masterpiece that tracks her descent with Walt into the underworld)
becomes a very literal "dip". Walt's transformation from suburban husband and
father to drug lord is reflected in a cake that is itself transformed from
sweetness to creepiness by the addition of a now infamous hat. Moments such as these
from the show have become shared cultural experiences, just as much as
the classics of baking have, passed down from generation to generation. And when
the two collide, they say interesting things about each other.

At the least, I hope my fellow fans will find solace in the warm, doughy delights
herein, and should anyone related to the show stumble across it they will enjoy my
attempt to bring the art of baking to bear on the great art the show has given us.

The Author, August 2014

THE AUTHORS WOULD LIKE TO THANK THE FOLLOWING:

SUPPLY - DAVID TRUMPER

**DISTRIBUTION -
ANNA VALENTINE-JONES,
EMMA SMITH,
AND THE TEAM AT ORION**

**(CRIMINAL) LAWYER -
CATRIONA DURELL**

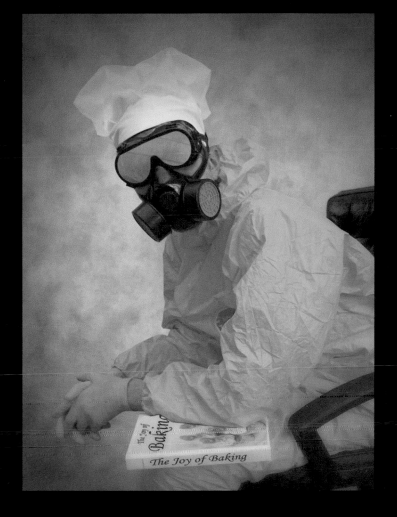

Walter Wheat is a retired Home Ec teacher and one of the greatest bakers in criminal history. Diagnosed with a terminal illness, he discovered a unique ability to produce restaurant-quality cupcakes for the black market. He is almost certainly dead

Remember my name...